SO-ACT-293

J 590 Min
Minden, Cecilia
Hard and soft

$12.79
ocn916684537

ANIMAL OPPOSITES
HARD AND SOFT

by Cecilia Minden

Cherry Lake Publishing • Ann Arbor, Michigan

Published in the United States of America
by Cherry Lake Publishing
Ann Arbor, Michigan
www.cherrylakepublishing.com

Reading Adviser: Marla Conn, ReadAbility, Inc.

Photo Credits: © Production Perig/Shutterstock Images, cover, 10;
© Kitch Bain/Shutterstock Images, 4; © Nneirda/Shutterstock Images, 6;
© Anneka/Shutterstock Images, 8; © Konrad Mostert/Shutterstock
Images, 12; © Mogens Trolle/Shutterstock Images, 14; © Graeme Knox/
Shutterstock Images, 16; © Kjersti Joergensen/Shutterstock Images, 18;
© Macjej Czekajewski/Shutterstock Images, 20; © Jennifer Nicole
Buchanan/Shutterstock Images, 20; © Arina P Habich/Shutterstock
Images, 20; © PCHT/Shutterstock Images, 20

Copyright ©2016 by Cherry Lake Publishing
All rights reserved. No part of this book may be reproduced or utilized in
any form or by any means without written permission from the publisher.

Library of Congress Cataloging-in-Publication Data
Hard and soft / by Cecilia Minden.
    pages cm.—(Animal opposites)
  Audience: K to grade 3.
  ISBN 978-1-63470-469-4 (hardcover)—ISBN 978-1-63470-589-9 (pbk.)—
ISBN 978-1-63470-529-5 (pdf)—ISBN 978-1-63470-649-0 (ebook)
 1. Animals—Juvenile literature. 2. Concepts—Juvenile literature.
3. Vocabulary. I. Title.
 QL49.M6735 2016
 590—dc23
                                                    2015025718

Cherry Lake Publishing would like to acknowledge
the work of the Partnership for 21st Century Skills.
Please visit *www.p21.org* for more information.

Printed in the United States of America
Corporate Graphics

TABLE OF CONTENTS

Pets

This **turtle** has a hard shell.
It keeps the turtle's body safe.

What Do You See?

What is the rabbit eating?

This **rabbit** has soft fur. It has a soft nose and soft ears.

Farm Animals

The egg is breaking open.
What is inside the hard shell?

It is a little chick. The chick has soft **down**.

What Do You See?

What are the rhinos doing?

Zoo Animals

Each rhino has a horn on its head. The horn is very hard.

A **zebra** has soft fur. It has black and white stripes.

Water Animals

This is a hard-shell **crab**. It likes to dig in the sand.

A **jellyfish** is soft, but it will sting!

Which animals are hard?

Which animals are soft?

Find Out More

BOOK

Horáček, Petr. *Animal Opposites.* Somerville, MA: Candlewick
    Press, 2013.

WEB SITE

The Activity Idea Place—Opposites
www.123child.com/lessonplans/other/opposites.php
Play some games to learn even more opposites.

Glossary

crab (KRAB) a creature that lives in water and has a hard shell, eight legs, and two claws

down (DOUN) the soft feathers of a bird

jellyfish (JEL-ee-fish) a sea creature with a soft body that can sometimes sting

rabbit (RAB-it) a soft, furry mammal with long ears that lives in a hole it digs in the ground

turtle (TUR-tuhl) a reptile that can pull its head, legs, and tail into its hard shell for protection

zebra (ZEE-bruh) a wild animal of southern and eastern Africa

Home and School Connection

Use this list of words from the book to help your child become a better reader. Word games and writing activities can help beginning readers reinforce literacy skills.

black	head	shell
body	horn	soft
breaking	inside	sting
chick	its	stripes
crab	jellyfish	the
dig	keeps	this
down	likes	turtle
each	little	turtle's
ears	nose	very
eating	open	water
egg	pets	what
farm	rabbit	white
fur	rhinos	will
hard	safe	zebra
has	sand	zoo

Harris County Public Library
Houston, Texas

Index

About the Author

Cecilia Minden, PhD, is a former classroom teacher and university professor. She now enjoys working as an educational consultant and writer for school and library publications. She has written more than 150 books for children. Cecilia lives in and out, up and down, and fast and slow in McKinney, Texas.